The Cookie Swap Cookbook

The Cookie Swap Cookbook

An irresistible collection of 80
cookie recipes to bake and share

This edition published in 2012
LOVE FOOD is an imprint of Parragon Books Ltd

Parragon
Queen Street House
4 Queen Street
Bath BA1 1HE, UK

LOVE FOOD and the accompanying heart device is a registered trademark of
Parragon Books Ltd in Australia, the UK, USA, India, and the EU.

www.parragon.com

ISBN: 978-1-4454-8201-9

Printed in China

Cover design by Talking Design

Notes for the Reader
This book uses standard kitchen measuring spoons and cups. All spoon and
cup measurements are level unless otherwise indicated. Unless otherwise
stated, milk is assumed to be whole, eggs are large, individual vegetables
are medium, and pepper is freshly ground black pepper. Unless otherwise
stated, all root vegetables should be washed and peeled before using.

The times given are only an approximate guide. Preparation times differ
according to the techniques used by different people and the cooking
times may also vary from those given. Optional ingredients, variations,
or serving suggestions have not been included in the calculations.

Recipes using raw or very lightly cooked eggs should be avoided by
infants, the elderly, pregnant women, and anyone with a chronic illness.
Pregnant and breast-feeding women are advised to avoid eating peanuts
and peanut products. People with nut allergies should be aware that some
of the prepared ingredients used in the recipes in this book may contain
nuts. Always check the packaging before use.

CONTENTS

INTRODUCTION

There's nothing quite as enticing as the tantalizing aroma of freshly baked cookies. As soon as you bite into a moist, warm home-baked cookie, you realize just how much more delicious they are than any store-bought versions. If you've never taken part in a cookie swap, and you're an ardent cookie lover, you don't know what you've been missing! It's a fantastic opportunity to share tasty treats and well-tested recipes with friends and family, and to discover a great selection of home-baked goodies that you're sure to make again and again.

Once you get the cookie bug, you will be eager to find new recipes and interesting twists on old favorites. With the huge variety of recipes available in this book, you'll be able to impress guests with all types of unusual flavors, from cookies for dunking in coffee to the perfect companion to a glass of milk. The only thing left to do will be to arrange a date to swap and exchange all kinds of delicious treats. The right packaging can transform your everyday baking—use the gift tags in this book to add a personal touch to your cookies, or try a simple length of ribbon or a pretty piece of paper to add a final flourish. Presentation is important at a cookie swap. If you're hosting, prepare platters to display all the baking to its best. For storage, remember to transfer the cookies from their display to an airtight jar, crisp plastic cellophane bag, or sealed container.

Organizing a Swap

Whether you're a seasoned swapper or new to the world of the cookie exchange, a few simple rules will make sure you have a smooth event every time:

• Calculate how many guests you plant to invite; consider friends, family, and neighbors—it's a great social event!

• Specify that all cookies must be homemade and baked; many established swaps stipulate no chocolate chip cookies, no-bakes, meringues, or bars, but you should decide what suits your guests' level of baking expertise.

• Consider how many cookies each swapper will need to bake and, equally, how many each guest will be able to take home.

• Send invitations! If you're planning your cookie swap far in advance, you should also send a save the date card.

• Always ask for an RSVP to your invitations, and remember to ask what each guest is baking, so that you can be sure there's no repetition.
• Remind guests to bring suitable containers for transporting their cookies home at the end of the swap.

Top Baking Hints & Tips

Once the party is organized, all that's left is to bake your cookies! Whether an experienced baker or a complete novice, here is some basic advice to keep your baking on track:
• Before you start to cook, read the recipe all the way through carefully. Collect all the ingredients and measure them out accurately.
• Preheat the oven to the required temperature.
• Do any chopping, slicing, or grating of the ingredients before you start mixing them.
• Don't take shortcuts: If the recipe asks you to chill the dough prior to cutting, do so—the dough will be easier to cut and the baked cookies will have a better finish.
• When making drop cookies, leave enough space between each cookie to allow for expansion during cooking, otherwise you'll end up with one large cookie!

• Cookies are soft when they come out of the oven, so let them cool slightly on the cookie sheet before transferring them to a wire rack to cool completely.
• Always store cookies in an airtight container, separate from cakes—cookies will absorb the moisture from cakes, leaving you with soggy cookies and dried-out cakes!
To avoid a last-minute rush before the occasion, make your cookie dough before the party. Wrap the dough tightly in plastic wrap and chill in the refrigerator, then place in a freezer-proof bag and transfer to the freezer. Drop cookies can be frozen on cookie sheets, then placed in freezer-proof bags and transferred to the freezer. Cookie dough will keep well in the freezer for 4–6 weeks. When you remove the dough from the freezer, let it stand at room temperature for 30 minutes before baking.

Use the tips and variations that accompany many of the following cookie recipes to add a new twist to old favorites—try adding golden raisins to Classic Oatmeal Cookies or add chopped caramels to the Mega Chip Cookies—swap dried fruits and nuts into the recipes to suit your taste.

Baking cookies is creative, enjoyable, and simple—it is a great way to create something really delicious in a short space of time. Get your invitations in the mail and let the fun begin!

Classic Favorites

Chocolate Chip Cookies

Makes 8

unsalted butter, melted,
  for greasing

1¼ cups all-purpose flour, sifted

1 tsp baking powder

½ cup margarine, melted

scant ½ cup light brown sugar

¼ cup superfine sugar

1 egg

⅔ cup semisweet chocolate chips

Preheat the oven to 375°F/190°C. Grease two baking sheets and line with parchment paper.

Place all of the ingredients in a large mixing bowl and beat until well combined.

Place tablespoonfuls of the mixture on the prepared baking sheets, spaced well apart.

Bake in the preheated oven for 10–12 minutes, or until golden brown. Transfer to a wire rack and let cool.

variation
use milk chocolate chips
instead of semisweet
if preferred

Classic Oatmeal Cookies

Makes 30

¾ cup butter or margarine,
   softened, plus extra
   for greasing
1⅓ cups raw brown sugar
1 egg
4 tbsp water
1 tsp vanilla extract
scant 4½ cups rolled oats
1 cup all-purpose flour
1 tsp salt
½ tsp baking soda

Preheat the oven to 350°F/180°C. Grease two large baking sheets.

Place the butter and sugar in a large bowl and beat together until light and fluffy. Beat in the egg, water, and vanilla extract until the mixture is smooth. Mix the oats, flour, salt, and baking soda together in a separate bowl, then gradually stir the oat mixture into the creamed mixture until thoroughly combined.

Place tablespoonfuls of the dough on the prepared baking sheets, spaced well apart.

Bake in the preheated oven for 15 minutes, or until golden brown. Transfer to a wire rack to cool completely.

variation
add golden raisins to the
dough mix

White Chocolate Cookies

Makes 24

½ cup butter, softened,
    plus extra for greasing
heaping ½ cup light brown sugar
1 egg, lightly beaten
heaping 1¾ cups self-rising flour
pinch of salt
4½ oz/125 g white chocolate,
    chopped
⅓ cup chopped Brazil nuts

Preheat the oven to 375°F/190°C. Grease several large baking sheets.

Place the butter and sugar in a large bowl and beat together until light and fluffy. Gradually add the egg, beating well after each addition.

Sift the flour and a pinch of salt into the creamed mixture and blend well. Stir in the chocolate and chopped nuts.

Place heaping teaspoonfuls of the mixture on the prepared baking sheets, putting no more than six on each sheet because the cookies will spread during cooking.

Bake in the preheated oven for 10–12 minutes, or until just golden brown. Transfer the cookies to wire racks to cool completely.

great tip!
chop chocolate
with a warm
knife to make easier

Simple Butter Cookies

Makes 25

1¼ cups all-purpose flour,
   plus extra for dusting

¼ tsp ground nutmeg

½ cup unsalted butter

¼ cup superfine sugar

Preheat the oven to 350°F/180°C. Sift the flour and nutmeg into a large bowl.

Add the butter and rub it into the mixture until it resembles breadcrumbs. Add the sugar and knead together to form a stiff dough.

Roll the dough out on a lightly floured work surface to about ¼ inch/5 mm thick.

Using a 2¾-inch/7-cm round cookie cutter dipped in flour, cut out 25 cookies. Reroll any trimmings. Place the cookies on two large nonstick baking sheets.

Bake in the preheated oven for 8–10 minutes, or until pale golden. Transfer to a wire rack and let cool completely.

variation
add a sprinkle of
cinnamon to create spice

Oat, Raisin & Hazelnut Cookies

Makes about 30

scant ½ cup raisins, chopped

½ cup orange juice

1 cup butter, softened

scant ¾ cup superfine sugar

1 egg yolk, lightly beaten

2 tsp vanilla extract

2 cups all-purpose flour

pinch of salt

½ cup rolled oats

½ cup chopped hazelnuts

whole hazelnuts, to decorate

Preheat the oven to 375°F/190°C. Line two baking sheets with parchment paper.

Put the raisins in a bowl, add the orange juice, and let soak for 10 minutes.

Put the butter and sugar into a bowl and mix well with a wooden spoon, then beat in the egg yolk and vanilla extract.

Sift together the flour and a pinch of salt into the mixture and add the oats and chopped hazelnuts. Drain the raisins, add them to the mixture, and stir until thoroughly combined.

Scoop up tablespoons of the mixture and put them in mounds on the prepared baking sheets, spaced well apart. Flatten slightly and place a whole hazelnut in the center of each cookie.

Bake in the preheated oven for 12–15 minutes, until golden brown. Let cool on the baking sheets for 5–10 minutes, then, using a metal spatula, carefully transfer the cookies to wire racks to cool completely.

Peanut Butter Cookies

Makes 12–15

1½ cups all-purpose flour

½ tsp baking powder

½ tsp salt

1 cup creamy peanut butter

½ cup butter, softened

1¼ tsp vanilla extract

½ cup light brown sugar

½ cup granulated sugar

2 eggs

Preheat the oven to 350°F/180°C. Sift together the flour, baking powder, and salt in a mixing bowl. In another large mixing bowl, cream the peanut butter, butter, and vanilla together until smooth. Add the sugars, and cream for one more minute. Mix in the eggs one at a time. Mix in the flour mixture, half at a time.

Wrap the dough in plastic wrap and refrigerate for at least 2 hours. Once chilled, roll or scoop the dough into 1½-inch/4-cm balls, and place on an ungreased, nonstick baking sheet, spaced well apart.

Use a fork to flatten each ball by making a crisscross pattern. Bake in the preheated oven for 15 minutes or until golden. Remove cookies from oven, and let cool on the baking sheet for 5 minutes. Using a metal spatula, transfer the cookies to a wire rack and let cool.

Spiced Rum Cookies

Makes 18

¾ cup unsalted butter, softened,
    plus extra for greasing
1 cup dark brown sugar
2 cups all-purpose flour
pinch of salt
½ tsp baking soda
1 tsp ground cinnamon
½ tsp ground coriander
½ tsp ground nutmeg
¼ tsp ground cloves
2 tbsp dark rum

Preheat the oven to 350°F/180°C. Grease two baking sheets.

Cream together the butter and sugar and whisk until light and fluffy.

Sift together the flour, a pinch of salt, baking soda, cinnamon, coriander, nutmeg, and cloves into the creamed mixture. Pour the dark rum into the creamed mixture and stir well.

Using two teaspoons, place small mounds of the mixture on the prepared baking sheets, spaced well apart. Flatten each one slightly with the back of a spoon.

Bake in the preheated oven for 10–12 minutes, or until golden. Let the cookies cool and become crisp on wire racks before serving.

variation
add raisins to dough
to create rum & raisin cookies

Cookies &
Cream Sandwiches

Makes about 15

generous ½ cup butter, softened

⅔ cup confectioners' sugar

heaping ¾ cup all-purpose flour

½ cup unsweetened cocoa

½ tsp ground cinnamon

Filling

4 oz/125 g semisweet chocolate,
    broken into pieces

¼ cup heavy cream

Preheat the oven to 325°F/160°C. Line two large baking sheets with parchment paper.

Place the butter and sugar in a large bowl and beat together until light and fluffy. Sift together the flour, cocoa, and cinnamon into the mixture and mix to form a dough.

Place the dough between two sheets of parchment paper and roll out until the dough is ⅛ inch/3 mm thick. Cut out 2½-inch/6-cm rounds and place on the prepared baking sheets.

Bake in the preheated oven for 15 minutes, or until firm to the touch. Let cool for 2 minutes on the parchment paper, then transfer the cookies to wire racks to cool completely.

Meanwhile, make the filling. Place the chocolate and cream in a saucepan and heat gently until the chocolate has melted. Stir until smooth. Let cool, then chill in the refrigerator for 2 hours, or until firm. Sandwich the cookies together in pairs with a spoonful of the chocolate cream and serve.

Gingersnaps

Makes 30

2½ cups self-rising flour

pinch of salt

1 cup superfine sugar

1 tbsp ground ginger

1 tsp baking soda

½ cup butter, plus extra
   for greasing

¼ cup dark corn syrup

1 egg, lightly beaten

1 tsp grated orange rind

Preheat the oven to 325°F/160°C. Grease several baking sheets.

Sift together the flour, a pinch of salt, sugar, ground ginger, and baking soda into a large mixing bowl.

Heat the butter and corn syrup together in a saucepan over very low heat until the butter has melted.

Let the butter mixture cool slightly, then pour it onto the dry ingredients. Add the egg and orange rind and mix together thoroughly.

Using your hands, carefully shape the dough into 30 even-size balls. Place the balls on the prepared baking sheets, spaced well apart, then flatten them slightly with your fingers.

Bake in the preheated oven for 15–20 minutes. Carefully transfer the cookies to a wire rack to cool and crisp.

Double Chocolate Cookies

Makes about 30

1 cup butter, softened

scant ¾ cup superfine sugar

1 egg yolk, lightly beaten

2 tsp vanilla extract

2¼ cups all-purpose flour

¼ cup unsweetened cocoa

pinch of salt

12 oz/350 g bittersweet
   chocolate, chopped

¼ cup dried sour cherries

Preheat the oven to 375°F/190°C. Line two baking sheets with parchment paper.

Put the butter and sugar into a bowl and mix well with a wooden spoon, then beat in the egg yolk and vanilla extract. Sift together the flour, cocoa, and a pinch of salt into the mixture, add the chopped chocolate and sour cherries, and stir until thoroughly combined.

Scoop up tablespoons of the mixture and shape into balls. Put them on the prepared baking sheets, spaced well apart, and flatten slightly.

Bake in the preheated oven for 12–15 minutes. Let cool on the baking sheets for 5–10 minutes, then, using a metal spatula, carefully transfer to wire racks to cool completely.

variation
replace bittersweet chocolate with milk chocolate if preferred

Cinnamon & Caramel Cookies

Makes about 25

1 cup butter, softened

scant ¾ cup superfine sugar

1 egg yolk, lightly beaten

1 tsp vanilla extract

2½ cups all-purpose flour

1 tsp ground cinnamon

½ tsp allspice

pinch of salt

25–30 hard caramel candies

Preheat the oven to 375°F/190°C. Line two baking sheets with parchment paper.

Put the butter and sugar into a bowl and mix well with a wooden spoon, then beat in the egg yolk and vanilla extract. Sift together the flour, cinnamon, allspice, and a pinch of salt into the mixture and stir until thoroughly combined.

Scoop up tablespoons of the mixture, shape into balls, and put on the prepared baking sheets, spaced well apart. Bake in the preheated oven for 8 minutes. Place a caramel candy on top of each cookie, return to the oven, and bake for an additional 6–7 minutes.

Remove from the oven and let cool on the baking sheets for 5–10 minutes. Using a metal spatula, carefully transfer the cookies to wire racks to cool completely.

variation
replace the caramel candies
with chocolate buttons

Mini Florentines

Makes 20–30

5½ tbsp butter

⅓ cup superfine sugar

2 tbsp golden raisins or raisins

3 tbsp candied cherries, chopped

1 tbsp finely chopped
    preserved ginger

3 tbsp sunflower seeds

scant 1 cup slivered almonds

2 tbsp heavy cream

6 oz/175 g semisweet or milk
    chocolate, broken into pieces

Preheat the oven to 350°F/180°C. Line two baking sheets with parchment paper. Place the butter in a small saucepan and melt over low heat. Add the sugar, stir until dissolved, then bring to a boil. Remove from the heat and stir in the golden raisins, candied cherries, preserved ginger, sunflower seeds, and almonds. Mix well, then beat in the cream.

Place teaspoons of the mixture on the prepared baking sheets, spaced well apart. Bake in the preheated oven for 10–12 minutes, or until light golden brown.

Remove from the oven and, while still hot, use a circular cookie cutter to pull in the edges to form circles. Let cool and become crisp before removing from the baking sheets.

Put the chocolate in a heatproof bowl set over a saucepan of gently simmering water and stir until melted. Spread most of the chocolate onto a sheet of parchment paper. When the chocolate is nearly set, place the cookies in the chocolate and let set. Cut around the florentines and remove from the parchment paper. Spread the remaining chocolate on the coated side of the florentines, using a fork to mark waves. Let set.

Sticky Ginger Cookies

Makes 20

1 cup butter, softened

scant ¾ cup superfine sugar

1 egg yolk, lightly beaten

¼ cup coarsely chopped preserved
   ginger, plus 1 tbsp syrup from
   the jar

2½ cups all-purpose flour

pinch of salt

⅓ cup semisweet chocolate chips

Put the butter and sugar into a bowl and mix well with a wooden spoon, then beat in the egg yolk and ginger syrup. Sift together the flour and a pinch of salt into the mixture, add the preserved ginger and chocolate chips, and stir until thoroughly combined.

Shape the mixture into a log, wrap in plastic wrap, and chill in the refrigerator for 30–60 minutes.

Preheat the oven to 375°F/190°C. Line two baking sheets with parchment paper.

Unwrap the log and cut it into ¼-inch/ 5-mm thick slices with a sharp serrated knife. Put them on the prepared baking sheets, spaced well apart.

Bake in the preheated oven for 12–15 minutes, until golden brown. Let cool on the baking sheets for 5–10 minutes, then, using a metal spatula, carefully transfer the cookies to wire racks to cool completely.

Almond Crunchies

Makes about 50

1 cup butter, softened

scant ¾ cup superfine sugar

1 egg yolk, lightly beaten

½ tsp almond extract

2 cups all-purpose flour

pinch of salt

2 cups blanched almonds,
  chopped

Put the butter and sugar into a bowl and mix well with a wooden spoon, then beat in the egg yolk and almond extract. Sift together the flour and a pinch of salt into the mixture, add the almonds, and stir until thoroughly combined. Halve the dough, shape it into balls, wrap in plastic wrap, and chill in the refrigerator for 30–60 minutes.

Preheat the oven to 375°F/190°C. Line two to three baking sheets with parchment paper.

Shape the dough into about 50 small balls and flatten them slightly between the palms of your hands. Put on the prepared baking sheets, spaced well apart. Bake in the preheated oven for 15–20 minutes, until golden brown. Let cool on the baking sheets for 5–10 minutes, then, using a metal spatula, carefully transfer to wire racks to cool completely.

variation
press marzipan into the middle of each cookie before cooking

Jelly Rings

Makes about 15

1 cup butter, softened

scant ¾ cup superfine sugar,
   plus extra for sprinkling

1 egg yolk, lightly beaten

2 tsp vanilla extract

2½ cups all-purpose flour

pinch of salt

1 egg white, lightly beaten

Jelly filling

4 tbsp butter, softened

scant 1 cup confectioners' sugar

5 tbsp strawberry or
   raspberry jelly

Put the butter and superfine sugar into a bowl and mix well, then beat in the egg yolk and vanilla extract. Sift together the flour and a pinch of salt into the mixture and stir until thoroughly combined. Halve the dough, shape into balls, wrap in plastic wrap, and chill for 30–60 minutes.

Preheat the oven to 375°F/190°C. Line two baking sheets with parchment paper. Unwrap the dough and roll out between two sheets of parchment paper. Stamp out cookies with a 2¾-inch/7-cm fluted round cutter and put half of them on a prepared baking sheet, spaced well apart. Using a 1½-inch/4-cm plain round cutter, stamp out the centers of the remaining cookies and remove. Put the cookie rings on the other baking sheet, spaced well apart.

Bake for 7 minutes, then brush the cookie rings with beaten egg white and sprinkle with superfine sugar. Bake for an additional 5–8 minutes, until light golden brown. Let cool on the baking sheets for 5–10 minutes, then transfer to wire racks to cool completely. To make the filling, beat the butter and confectioners' sugar together in a bowl. Spread the buttercream over the whole cookies and top with jelly. Place the cookie rings on top and press together.

Biscotti

Makes about 30

1 cup butter, softened

scant ¾ cup superfine sugar

finely grated rind of 1 lemon

1 egg yolk, lightly beaten

2 tsp brandy

2½ cups all-purpose flour

pinch of salt

¾ cup pistachios

confectioners' sugar,
   for dusting

Put the butter, superfine sugar, and lemon rind into a bowl and mix well with a wooden spoon, then beat in the egg yolk and brandy. Sift the flour and a pinch of salt into the mixture, add the pistachios, and stir until thoroughly combined.

Shape the mixture into a log, flatten slightly, wrap in plastic wrap, and chill in the refrigerator for 30–60 minutes.

Preheat the oven to 375°F/190°C. Line two baking sheets with parchment paper.

Unwrap the log and cut it slightly on the diagonal into ¼-inch/5-mm thick slices with a sharp serrated knife. Put them on the prepared baking sheets, spaced well apart.

Bake in the preheated oven for 10 minutes, until golden brown. Using a metal spatula, carefully transfer the cookies to wire racks. Dust with confectioners' sugar and let cool.

Mixed Fruit Cookies

Makes about 30

1 cup butter, softened

scant ¾ cup superfine sugar

1 egg yolk, lightly beaten

2½ cups all-purpose flour

½ tsp apple pie spice

pinch of salt

¼ cup chopped plumped
   dried apple

¼ cup chopped plumped
   dried pear

¼ cup chopped plumped
   dried plums (prunes)

grated rind of 1 orange

Put the butter and sugar into a bowl and mix well with a wooden spoon, then beat in the egg yolk. Sift together the flour, apple pie spice, and a pinch of salt into the mixture. Add the apple, pear, prunes, and orange rind, and stir until thoroughly combined. Shape the dough into a log, wrap in plastic wrap, and chill in the refrigerator for 30–60 minutes.

Preheat the oven to 375°F/190°C. Line two baking sheets with parchment paper.

Unwrap the log and cut it into ¼-inch/ 5-mm thick slices with a sharp serrated knife. Put them on the prepared baking sheets, spaced well apart.

Bake in the preheated oven for 10–15 minutes, until golden brown. Let cool on the baking sheets for 5–10 minutes, then, using a metal spatula, carefully transfer the cookies to wire racks to cool completely.

Butter Cookies

Makes 25

generous ½ cup unsalted butter, softened

⅔ cup superfine sugar

1 extra large egg yolk

¾ cup all-purpose flour

1 tsp ground cinnamon

Preheat the oven to 400°F/200°C. Line a large baking sheet with parchment paper.

Place the butter and 2 tablespoons of the sugar in a large bowl and beat together until light and fluffy. Add the egg yolk and stir together, then sift in the flour and mix to form a soft dough.

Mix the remaining sugar with the cinnamon. Take a teaspoon of dough and roll it in the sugar mixture. Place on the prepared baking sheet and use a fork to press down until the cookie is ½ inch/1 cm thick. Repeat until all the dough is used up.

Bake in the preheated oven for 10 minutes, or until golden brown. Transfer to a wire rack to cool completely.

variation
add scant 1 cup dry unsweetened shredded coconut to dough and omit the cinnamon

Good-For-You Whole Wheat Cookies

Makes 36

2¼ cups whole wheat flour,
   plus extra for dusting

2 tbsp wheat germ

¼ tsp baking soda

½ tsp salt

¼ cup superfine sugar

generous ½ cup unsalted butter,
   softened, cubed

1 extra large egg, lightly beaten

1 tsp vanilla extract

Preheat the oven to 325°F/160°C.

Place the flour, wheat germ, baking soda, salt, and sugar in a large bowl and stir together until combined. Add the butter and rub it in until the mixture resembles breadcrumbs.

Whisk the egg and vanilla extract in a separate bowl and add to the mixture, adding a little cold water if needed to bring the dough together. Roll the dough out on a floured board. Use a 2¾-inch/7-cm floured cookie cutter to cut out the cookies and place them on nonstick baking sheets, rerolling the dough when necessary.

Bake in the preheated oven for 20–25 minutes, or until dry but not brown. Transfer to a wire rack to cool completely.

variation
add 2 tbsp of chopped
currants to the dough

Chocolate Orange Cookies

Makes 30

scant ½ cup butter, softened

⅓ cup superfine sugar

1 egg

1 tbsp milk

2 cups all-purpose flour,
   plus extra for dusting

2 tbsp unsweetened cocoa

To decorate

1½ cups confectioners' sugar

3 tbsp orange juice

a little semisweet chocolate,
   broken into pieces

Preheat the oven to 350°F/180°C. Line two large baking sheets with parchment paper. Place the butter and superfine sugar in a large bowl and beat together until light and fluffy. Beat in the egg and milk until thoroughly combined. Sift the flour and cocoa into the bowl and gradually mix together to form a soft dough.

Roll out the dough on a lightly floured work surface until it is about ¼-inch/5-mm thick. Cut out rounds with a 2-inch/5-cm fluted round cookie cutter and place them on the prepared baking sheets. Bake in the preheated oven for 10–12 minutes, or until golden. Let cool on the baking sheet for a few minutes, then transfer the cookies to a wire rack to cool completely and become crisp.

To make the icing, sift the confectioners' sugar in a bowl and stir in enough orange juice to form a thin icing that will coat the back of the spoon. Place a spoonful of icing in the center of each cookie and let set.

Place the chocolate in a heatproof bowl, set the bowl over a saucepan of gently simmering water, and heat until melted. Drizzle thin lines of melted chocolate over the cookies and let set before serving.

Chocolate
Choice

Mega Chip Cookies

Makes 12

1 cup butter, softened

scant ¾ cup superfine sugar

1 egg yolk, lightly beaten

2 tsp vanilla extract

2 cups all-purpose flour

½ cup unsweetened cocoa

pinch of salt

½ cup milk chocolate chips

½ cup white chocolate chips

4 oz/115 g bittersweet chocolate,
   coarsely chopped

Preheat the oven to 375°F/190°C.
Line two to three baking sheets with
parchment paper.

Put the butter and sugar into a bowl and
mix well with a wooden spoon, then beat in
the egg yolk and vanilla extract. Sift together
the flour, cocoa, and a pinch of salt into the
mixture, add both kinds of chocolate chips,
and stir until thoroughly combined.

Make 12 balls of the mixture, put them
on the prepared baking sheets, spaced well
apart, and flatten slightly. Press the pieces of
bittersweet chocolate into the cookies.

Bake in the preheated oven for
12–15 minutes. Let cool on the baking
sheets for 5–10 minutes, then, using a metal
spatula, carefully transfer to wire racks to
cool completely.

variation
replace a variety of
chocolate chip with
chopped caramels

Chocolate Chip & Cinnamon Cookies

Makes about 30

1 cup butter, softened

scant ¾ cup superfine sugar

1 egg yolk, lightly beaten

2 tsp orange extract

2½ cups all-purpose flour

pinch of salt

heaping ½ cup semisweet
  chocolate chips

Cinnamon coating

1½ tbsp superfine sugar

1½ tbsp ground cinnamon

Preheat the oven to 375°F/190°C. Line two baking sheets with parchment paper.

Put the butter and sugar into a bowl and mix well with a wooden spoon, then beat in the egg yolk and orange extract. Sift together the flour and a pinch of salt into the mixture, add the chocolate chips, and stir until thoroughly combined.

For the coating, mix together the sugar and cinnamon in a shallow dish. Scoop out tablespoons of the cookie dough, roll them into balls, then roll them in the cinnamon mixture to coat. Put them on the prepared baking sheets, spaced well apart.

Bake in the preheated oven for 12–15 minutes. Let cool on the baking sheets for 5–10 minutes, then, using a metal spatula, carefully transfer to wire racks to cool completely.

variation
*use white chocolate chips
instead of semisweet*

Midnight Cookies

Makes 25

generous ½ cup butter, softened

1 cup superfine sugar

1 egg, lightly beaten

½ tsp vanilla extract

1 cup all-purpose flour

⅓ cup unsweetened cocoa

½ tsp baking soda

Preheat the oven to 350°F/180°C. Line several large baking sheets with parchment paper.

Place the butter and sugar in a large bowl and beat together until light and fluffy. Add the egg and vanilla extract and mix until smooth. Sift in the flour, cocoa, and baking soda and beat until well mixed.

With dampened hands, roll walnut-size pieces of the dough into smooth balls. Place on the prepared baking sheets, spaced well apart.

Bake in the preheated oven for 10–12 minutes, or until set. Let cool on the baking sheets for 5 minutes, then transfer the cookies to wire racks to cool completely before serving.

variation
for a sugar coating, roll each cookie dough ball in sugar

Chocolate Mint Cookie Sandwiches

Makes about 15

1 cup butter, softened

scant ¾ cup superfine sugar

1 egg yolk, lightly beaten

2 tsp vanilla extract

2¼ cups all-purpose flour

½ cup unsweetened cocoa

pinch of salt

⅓ cup candied cherries,
   finely chopped

15 after-dinner mints

Chocolate coating

4 oz/115 g semisweet chocolate,
   broken into pieces

2 oz/55 g white chocolate,
   broken into pieces

Put the butter and sugar into a bowl and mix well with a wooden spoon, then beat in the egg yolk and vanilla extract. Sift together the flour, cocoa, and a pinch of salt into the mixture, add the cherries, and stir. Halve the dough, shape into balls, wrap in plastic wrap, and chill in the refrigerator for 30–60 minutes.

Preheat the oven to 375°F/190°C. Line two baking sheets with parchment paper. Unwrap the dough and roll out between two sheets of parchment paper. Stamp out cookies with a 2½-inch/6-cm plain square cutter and put them on the prepared baking sheets, spaced well apart. Bake in the preheated oven for 10–15 minutes, until firm. Place an after-dinner mint on top of half the cookies, then cover with the remaining cookies. Press down gently and let cool.

For the chocolate coating, melt the semisweet chocolate in a heatproof bowl set over a saucepan of simmering water. Remove from the heat and let cool. Put the cookies on a wire rack over a sheet of parchment paper. Spoon the semisweet chocolate over them, then tap the rack to level the surface, and let set. Melt the white chocolate in a heatproof bowl set over a saucepan of simmering water. Remove from the heat and let cool. Pipe over the cookies, then let set.

Chocolate & Orange Cookie Sandwiches

Makes about 15

1 cup butter, softened

scant ¾ cup superfine sugar

2 tsp finely grated orange rind

1 egg yolk, lightly beaten

2 tsp vanilla extract

2¼ cups all-purpose flour

¼ cup unsweetened cocoa

pinch of salt

3½ oz/100 g semisweet chocolate,
    finely chopped

Filling

½ cup heavy cream

7 oz/200 g white chocolate,
    broken into pieces

1 tsp orange extract

Preheat the oven to 375°F/190°C. Line two baking sheets with parchment paper.

Put the butter, sugar, and orange rind into a bowl and mix well with a wooden spoon, then beat in the egg yolk and vanilla extract. Sift together the flour, cocoa, and a pinch of salt into the mixture, add the semisweet chocolate, and stir until thoroughly combined.

Scoop up tablespoons of the dough, roll into balls, and put on the prepared baking sheets, spaced well apart. Gently flatten and smooth the tops with the back of a spoon.

Bake in the preheated oven for 10–15 minutes, until light golden brown. Let cool on the baking sheets for 5–10 minutes, then, using a metal spatula, carefully transfer to wire racks to cool completely.

To make the filling, bring the cream to a boil in a small saucepan, then remove the saucepan from the heat. Stir in the white chocolate until the mixture is smooth, then stir in the orange extract. When the mixture is completely cool, use to sandwich the cookies together in pairs.

Mocha Walnut Cookies

Makes about 16

½ cup butter, softened,
    plus extra for greasing
heaping ½ cup dark brown sugar
scant ½ cup superfine sugar
1 tsp vanilla extract
1 tbsp instant coffee powder,
    dissolved in 1 tbsp hot water
1 egg
1¼ cups all-purpose flour
½ tsp baking powder
¼ tsp baking soda
⅓ cup milk chocolate chips
½ cup walnut halves,
    coarsely chopped

Preheat the oven to 350°F/180°C. Grease two large baking sheets. Place the butter and sugars in a large bowl and beat together until light and fluffy.

Place the vanilla, coffee, and egg in a separate bowl and whisk together. Gradually add the coffee mixture to the butter and sugar, beating until fluffy. Sift the flour, baking powder, and baking soda into the mixture and fold in carefully. Fold in the chocolate chips and walnuts.

Spoon heaping teaspoons of the dough on the prepared baking sheets, spaced well apart. Bake in the preheated oven for 10–15 minutes, or until crisp on the outside but soft inside. Let cool on the baking sheets for 2 minutes, then transfer to wire racks to cool completely.

variation
add slivered almonds instead of walnuts

Chocolate Sprinkle Cookies

Makes about 30

1 cup butter, softened

scant ¾ cup superfine sugar

1 egg yolk, lightly beaten

2 tsp vanilla extract

2 cups all-purpose flour,
   plus extra for dusting

½ cup unsweetened cocoa

pinch of salt

To decorate

7 oz/200 g white chocolate,
   broken into pieces

⅓ cup chocolate sprinkles

Put the butter and sugar into a bowl and mix well with a wooden spoon, then beat in the egg yolk and vanilla extract. Sift together the flour, cocoa, and a pinch of salt into the mixture and stir until thoroughly combined. Halve the dough, roll each piece into a ball, wrap in plastic wrap, and chill in the refrigerator for 30–60 minutes.

Preheat the oven to 375°F/190°C. Line two baking sheets with parchment paper. Unwrap the dough and roll out between two sheets of parchment paper to about ¼ inch/5 mm thick and stamp out 30 cookies with a 2½–2¾-inch/6–7-cm fluted round cutter. Put them on the prepared baking sheets, spaced well apart.

Bake in the preheated oven for 10–12 minutes. Let cool on the baking sheets for 5–10 minutes, then, using a metal spatula, carefully transfer the cookies to wire racks to cool completely. Put the pieces of white chocolate into a heatproof bowl and melt over a saucepan of gently simmering water, then immediately remove from the heat. Spread the melted chocolate over the cookies, let cool slightly, and then sprinkle with the chocolate sprinkles. Let cool and set.

Chocolate Fudge Squares

Makes about 30

1 cup butter, softened

scant ¾ cup superfine sugar

1 egg yolk, lightly beaten

2 tsp vanilla extract

2 cups all-purpose flour

½ cup unsweetened cocoa

pinch of salt

Chocolate fudge topping

8 chocolate-coated fudge fingers,
   broken into pieces

4 tbsp heavy cream

Put the butter and sugar into a bowl and mix well with a wooden spoon, then beat in the egg yolk and vanilla extract. Sift together the flour, cocoa, and a pinch of salt into the mixture and stir until thoroughly combined. Halve the dough, shape into balls, wrap in plastic wrap, and chill in the refrigerator for 30–60 minutes. Preheat the oven to 375°F/190°C. Line two baking sheets with parchment paper.

Unwrap the dough and roll out between two sheets of parchment paper to about ⅛ inch/3 mm thick. Stamp out cookies with a 2½-inch/6-cm square cutter and put them on the prepared baking sheets, spaced well apart. Bake in the preheated oven for 10–15 minutes, until golden brown. Let cool on the baking sheets for 5–10 minutes, then, using a metal spatula, carefully transfer the cookies to wire racks to cool completely.

For the topping, put the fudge fingers into a heatproof bowl and melt over a saucepan of gently simmering water. Remove the bowl from the heat and gradually whisk in the cream. Let cool, then chill until spreadable. Spread the fudge topping over the cookies before serving.

Chocolate & Hazelnut Spread Drops

Makes about 30

1 cup butter, softened

scant ¾ cup superfine sugar

1 egg yolk, lightly beaten

2 tsp vanilla extract

2 cups all-purpose flour

½ cup unsweetened cocoa

pinch of salt

½ cup ground hazelnuts

⅓ cup semisweet chocolate chips

4 tbsp chocolate and hazelnut
    spread

Preheat the oven to 375°F/190°C. Line two baking sheets with parchment paper.

Put the butter and sugar into a bowl and mix well with a wooden spoon, then beat in the egg yolk and vanilla extract. Sift together the flour, cocoa, and a pinch of salt into the mixture, add the ground hazelnuts and chocolate chips, and stir until thoroughly combined.

Scoop out tablespoons of the mixture and shape into balls with your hands, then put them on the prepared baking sheets, spaced well apart. Use the dampened handle of a wooden spoon to make a hollow in the center of each cookie.

Bake in the preheated oven for 12–15 minutes. Let cool on the baking sheets for 5–10 minutes, then, using a metal spatula, carefully transfer the cookies to wire racks to cool completely. When they have cooled down completely, fill the hollows in the center with chocolate and hazelnut spread.

Chocolate Whole Wheat Cookies

Makes 20

5½ tbsp butter, softened,
    plus extra for greasing
scant ⅔ cup raw brown sugar
1 egg
1 tbsp wheat germ
1 cup whole wheat self-rising
    flour
½ cup self-rising flour
4½ oz/125 g semisweet
    chocolate, broken into pieces

Preheat the oven to 350°F/180°C. Grease two large baking sheets.

Place the butter and sugar in a large bowl and beat together until light and fluffy. Add the egg and beat well. Stir in the wheat germ and flours, then bring the mixture together with your hands. Roll rounded teaspoonfuls of the dough into balls and place them on the prepared baking sheets, spaced well apart, then flatten slightly with the tines of a fork.

Bake in the preheated oven for 15–20 minutes, or until golden brown. Let cool for a few minutes, then transfer the cookies to a wire rack to cool completely.

Place the chocolate in a heatproof bowl, set the bowl over a saucepan of gently simmering water, and heat until melted. Dip each cookie in the chocolate to cover the flat side and a little way around the edges. Let the excess drip back into the bowl. Place the cookies on a sheet of parchment paper in a cool place and let set before serving.

Chocolate & Apricot Cookies

Makes about 30

1 cup butter, softened

¾ cup superfine sugar

1 egg yolk, lightly beaten

2 tsp amaretto liqueur

2 cups all-purpose flour

pinch of salt

⅓ cup semisweet chocolate chips

⅓ cup plumped dried apricots, chopped

⅔ cup blanched almonds, chopped

Place the butter and sugar in a large bowl and beat together until light and fluffy, then beat in the egg yolk and amaretto liqueur. Sift together the flour and a pinch of salt into the mixture, add the chocolate chips and apricots, and stir until thoroughly combined.

Shape the mixture into a log. Spread out the almonds in a shallow dish and roll the log in them to coat. Wrap in plastic wrap and chill for 30–60 minutes.

Preheat the oven to 375°F/190°C. Line two large baking sheets with parchment paper. Unwrap the dough, cut into ¼-inch/5-mm thick slices with a sharp serrated knife, and place them on the prepared baking sheets, spaced well apart.

Bake in the preheated oven for 12–15 minutes, or until golden brown. Let cool for 5–10 minutes, then transfer the cookies to wire racks to cool completely.

White Chocolate & Plum Cookies

Makes about 30

1 cup butter, softened

¾ cup superfine sugar

1 egg yolk, lightly beaten

2 tsp vanilla extract

1⅔ cups all-purpose flour

½ cup unsweetened cocoa

pinch of salt

3½ oz/100 g white chocolate, chopped

To decorate

2 oz/55 g white chocolate, broken into pieces

15 plumped dried plums (prunes), halved

Place the butter and sugar in a large bowl and beat together until fluffy, then beat in the egg yolk and vanilla extract. Sift the flour, cocoa, and a pinch of salt into the mixture and stir. Halve the dough, shape into balls, wrap in plastic wrap, and chill for 30–60 minutes.

Preheat the oven to 375°F/190°C. Line two large baking sheets with parchment paper. Unwrap a ball of dough and roll out between two sheets of parchment paper to about ⅛ inch/3 mm thick. Cut out 15 rounds with a plain 2-inch/5-cm cutter and place them on the prepared baking sheets, spaced well apart. Divide the chopped chocolate among the cookies.

Roll out the remaining dough between two sheets of parchment paper and cut out rounds with a 2½–2¾-inch/6–7-cm cutter. Place them on top of the first cookies and press together to seal. Bake in the preheated oven for 10–15 minutes, until firm. Let cool for 5–10 minutes, then transfer the cookies to wire racks to cool completely. To decorate, place the chocolate in a heatproof bowl, set the bowl over a saucepan of simmering water, and heat until melted. Let cool. Dip the plums into the melted chocolate and place in the middle of the cookies. Spoon the remaining chocolate over them and let set.

Chocolate Party Cookies

Makes 15

scant ½ cup butter, softened

½ cup light brown sugar

1 tbsp dark corn syrup

heaping 1 cup self-rising flour

3 oz/85 g sugar-coated
   chocolates

Preheat the oven to 350°F/180°C. Line several large baking sheets with parchment paper. Place the butter and sugar in a large bowl and whisk together until pale and creamy, then whisk the dark corn syrup into the mixture until smooth. Add ½ cup flour and whisk together until mixed. Stir in the sugar-coated chocolates and remaining flour then, with your hands, knead the mixture until smooth.

Roll small pieces of the dough between your hands into smooth balls to make 15 cookies in total and place them on the prepared baking sheets, spaced well apart. Bake in the preheated oven for 10–15 minutes, or until golden brown.

Let cool on the baking sheets for 2–3 minutes, then transfer the cookies to a wire rack and let cool completely.

variation
use sugar-coated peanuts
instead

Choco Mint Stars

Makes about 30

1 cup butter, softened

¾ cup superfine sugar

1 egg yolk, lightly beaten

1 tsp peppermint extract

2 cups all-purpose flour

pinch of salt

heaping 1 cup dry unsweetened
   coconut

To decorate

3½ oz/100 g white chocolate,
   broken into pieces

3½ oz/100 g milk chocolate,
   broken into pieces

Place the butter and sugar in a large bowl and beat together until light and fluffy, then beat in the egg yolk and peppermint extract. Sift together the flour and a pinch of salt into the mixture, add the coconut, and stir until combined. Divide the mixture in half, shape into balls, wrap in plastic wrap, and chill for 30–60 minutes.

Preheat the oven to 375°F/190°C. Line two large baking sheets with parchment paper. Unwrap the dough and roll out between two sheets of parchment paper to about ⅛ inch/3 mm thick.

Cut out stars with a 2½–2¾-inch/6–7-cm cutter and place them on the prepared baking sheets, spaced well apart. Bake in the preheated oven for 10–12 minutes, or until light golden. Let cool on the baking sheets for 5–10 minutes, then transfer the cookies to wire racks to cool completely.

Place the white chocolate and the milk chocolate in separate heatproof bowls, set the bowls over two saucepans of gently simmering water, and heat until melted. Leave the cooled cookies on the racks and drizzle first with melted white chocolate and then with melted milk chocolate, using a teaspoon. Let set.

Giant Chocolate Chunk Cookies

Makes 12

½ cup butter, softened

scant ⅔ cup superfine sugar

scant ⅔ cup light brown sugar

2 extra large eggs, lightly beaten

1 tsp vanilla extract

2 cups all-purpose flour

1 tsp baking soda

10½ oz/300 g chocolate chunks

Preheat the oven to 350°F/180°C. Line several large baking sheets with parchment paper.

Place the butter and sugars in a large bowl and whisk together until pale and creamy. Whisk the eggs and vanilla extract into the mixture until smooth. Sift in the flour and baking soda and beat together until well mixed. Stir in the chocolate chunks.

Drop 12 large spoonfuls of the mixture on the prepared baking sheets, spaced well apart.

Bake in the preheated oven for 15–20 minutes, or until set and golden brown. Let cool on the baking sheets for 2–3 minutes, then transfer the cookies to a wire rack and let cool completely.

variation
use milk, white or bittersweet chocolate chunks for variety

Chocolate & Coffee Whole Wheat Cookies

Makes 24

scant ¾ cup butter, softened,
   plus extra for greasing
1 cup light brown sugar
1 egg
½ cup all-purpose flour, plus extra
   for dusting (optional)
1 tsp baking soda
pinch of salt
½ cup whole wheat flour
1 tbsp bran
heaping 1¼ cups semisweet
   chocolate chips
scant 2¼ cups rolled oats
1 tbsp strong coffee
⅔ cup hazelnuts, toasted
   and coarsely chopped

Preheat the oven to 375°F/190°C. Grease two large baking sheets. Place the butter and sugar in a large bowl and beat together until light and fluffy. Add the egg and beat well. Sift together the all-purpose flour, baking soda, and a pinch of salt into another bowl, then add in the whole wheat flour and bran. Mix in the egg mixture, then stir in the chocolate chips, oats, coffee, and hazelnuts and mix well.

Place 24 rounded tablespoons of the dough on the prepared baking sheets, spaced well apart. Alternatively, with lightly floured hands, break off pieces of the dough and roll into 24 balls, place on the prepared baking sheets, spaced well apart, and flatten.

Bake in the preheated oven for 16–18 minutes, or until golden brown. Let cool for 5 minutes, then transfer to a wire rack to cool completely.

great tip!
sandwich these cookies
together with chocolate
ice cream

Chocolate & Banana Cookies

Makes about 20

generous ½ cup butter, softened

⅔ cup superfine sugar

1 extra large egg, lightly beaten

1 ripe banana

1¼ cups self-rising flour

1 tsp apple pie spice

2 tbsp milk

3½ oz/100 g chocolate,
   cut into chunks

⅓ cup raisins

Preheat the oven to 375°F/190°C. Line two large baking sheets with parchment paper.

Place the butter and sugar in a large bowl and beat together until light and fluffy. Gradually add the egg, beating well after each addition. Mash the banana and add it to the mixture, beating well until smooth.

Sift together the flour and apple pie spice into the mixture and fold in with a spatula. Add the milk to produce a soft consistency, then fold in the chocolate and raisins. Drop tablespoons of the mixture on the prepared baking sheets, spaced well apart.

Bake in the preheated oven for 15–20 minutes, or until lightly golden. Let cool slightly, then transfer to a wire rack to cool completely.

variation
add toffee to the dough mix to create a chewier cookie

Chocolate & Almond Biscotti

Makes 24

butter, for greasing

1 cup blanched almonds

5½ oz/150 g semisweet chocolate, broken into pieces

heaping 1¾ cups all-purpose flour, plus extra for dusting

1 tsp baking powder

¾ cup superfine sugar

2 extra large eggs, lightly beaten

1 tsp vanilla extract

Preheat the oven to 325°F/160°C. Grease a large baking sheet. Spread the almonds on another baking sheet and bake in the preheated oven for 5–10 minutes, or until lightly toasted. Let cool.

Place the chocolate in a heatproof bowl, set the bowl over a saucepan of gently simmering water, and heat until melted. Remove from the heat and stir until smooth, then let cool. Sift the flour and baking powder into a large bowl. Add the sugar, cooled almonds, chocolate, eggs, and vanilla extract and mix together to form a soft dough. Turn the dough onto a lightly floured work surface and, with floured hands, knead for 2–3 minutes. Divide the dough in half and shape each portion into a log shape measuring about 2 inches/5 cm in diameter. Place the logs on the prepared baking sheet and flatten until each is 1 inch/2.5 cm thick.

Bake in the preheated oven for 20–30 minutes, or until firm to the touch. Let cool for 15 minutes. Reduce the oven temperature to 300°F/150°C. Using a serrated knife, cut the baked dough into ½-inch/1-cm thick slices and place on ungreased baking sheets. Bake in the oven for 10 minutes. Turn and bake for an additional 10–15 minutes. Transfer to a wire rack to cool.

Orange & Chocolate Fingers

Makes about 35

1 cup butter, softened

scant ¾ cup superfine sugar

grated rind of 1 orange

1 egg yolk, lightly beaten

2 tsp orange juice

2½ cups all-purpose flour

1 tsp ground ginger

pinch of salt

4 oz/115 g bittersweet chocolate,
  broken into pieces

Put the butter, sugar, and orange rind into a bowl and mix well with a wooden spoon, then beat in the egg yolk and orange juice. Sift together the flour, ginger, and a pinch of salt into the mixture and stir until thoroughly combined. Shape the dough into a ball, wrap in plastic wrap, and chill in the refrigerator for 30–60 minutes.

Preheat the oven to 375°F/190°C. Line two baking sheets with parchment paper. Unwrap the dough and roll out between two sheets of parchment paper to a rectangle. Using a sharp knife, cut it into 4 x ¾-inch/10 x 2-cm strips and put them on the prepared baking sheets, spaced well apart. Bake in the preheated oven for 10–12 minutes, until light golden brown. Let cool on the baking sheets for 5–10 minutes, then, using a metal spatula, carefully transfer to wire racks to cool completely.

Put the pieces of chocolate into a heatproof bowl and melt over a saucepan of gently simmering water, then remove from the heat and let cool. When the chocolate is cool but not set, dip the cookies diagonally into it to coat halfway, then put on the wire racks and let set. You may find it easier to do this using tongs.

Chocolate Buttons

Makes about 30

2 envelopes instant chocolate or
   fudge chocolate drink

1 tbsp hot water

1 cup butter, softened

scant ¾ cup superfine sugar,
   plus extra for sprinkling

1 egg yolk, lightly beaten

2½ cups all-purpose flour

pinch of salt

Empty the chocolate drink envelopes into a bowl and stir in the hot water to make a paste. Put the butter and sugar into a bowl and mix well with a wooden spoon, then beat in the egg yolk and chocolate paste. Sift together the flour and a pinch of salt into the mixture and stir until thoroughly combined. Halve the dough, shape into rounds, wrap in plastic wrap, and chill in the refrigerator for 30–60 minutes.

Preheat the oven to 375°F/190°C. Line two baking sheets with parchment paper.

Unwrap the dough and roll out between two sheets of parchment paper to ⅛ inch/ 3 mm thick. Stamp out cookies with a plain 2-inch/5-cm cutter. Using a 1¼-inch/3-cm cap from a soda or mineral water bottle, make an indentation in the center of each button. Using a wooden toothpick, make four holes in the center of each button, then put them on the prepared baking sheets, spaced well apart. Sprinkle with superfine sugar.

Bake in the preheated oven for 10–15 minutes, until firm. Let cool on the baking sheets for 5–10 minutes, then, using a metal spatula, transfer to wire racks to cool completely.

Fabulous Fruit & Nut

Coconut & Cranberry Cookies

Makes about 30

1 cup butter, softened

scant ¾ cup superfine sugar

1 egg yolk, lightly beaten

2 tsp vanilla extract

2½ cups all-purpose flour

pinch of salt

½ cup dry unsweetened coconut

½ cup dried cranberries

Preheat the oven to 375°F/190°C. Line two baking sheets with parchment paper.

Put the butter and sugar into a bowl and mix well with a wooden spoon, then beat in the egg yolk and vanilla extract. Sift together the flour and a pinch of salt into the mixture, add the coconut and cranberries, and stir until thoroughly combined.

Scoop up tablespoons of the dough and place in mounds on the prepared baking sheets, spaced well apart.

Bake in the preheated oven for 12–15 minutes, until golden brown. Let cool on the baking sheets for 5–10 minutes, then, using a metal spatula, carefully transfer to wire racks to cool completely.

variation
replace the cranberries
with dried blueberries

Walnut & Coffee Cookies

Makes about 30

2 envelopes instant latte

1 tbsp hot water

1 cup butter, softened

scant ¾ cup superfine sugar

1 egg yolk, lightly beaten

2½ cups all-purpose flour

pinch of salt

scant 1 cup finely
   chopped walnuts

sugar crystals, for sprinkling

Put the instant latte into a bowl and stir in the hot, but not boiling, water to make a paste. Put the butter and sugar into a bowl and mix well with a wooden spoon, then beat in the egg yolk and coffee paste. Sift together the flour and a pinch of salt into the mixture, add the walnuts, and stir until thoroughly combined. Halve the dough, shape into balls, wrap in plastic wrap, and chill in the refrigerator for 30–60 minutes.

Preheat the oven to 375°F/190°C. Line two baking sheets with parchment paper.

Unwrap the dough and roll out between two sheets of parchment paper to about ⅛ inch/3 mm thick. Stamp out cookies with a 2½-inch/6-cm round cutter and put them on the prepared baking sheets, spaced well apart.

Lightly brush the cookies with water, sprinkle with the sugar crystals, and bake in the preheated oven for 10–12 minutes. Let cool on the baking sheets for 5–10 minutes, then, using a metal spatula, carefully transfer the cookies to wire racks to cool completely.

Banana & Raisin Cookies

Makes about 30

scant ¼ cup raisins

½ cup orange juice or rum

1 cup butter, softened

scant ¾ cup superfine sugar

1 egg yolk, lightly beaten

2½ cups all-purpose flour

pinch of salt

¾ cup finely chopped dried banana

Put the raisins into a bowl, pour in the orange juice or rum, and let soak for 30 minutes. Drain the raisins, reserving any remaining orange juice or rum.

Preheat the oven to 375°F/190°C. Line two baking sheets with parchment paper.

Put the butter and sugar into a bowl and mix well with a wooden spoon, then beat in the egg yolk and 2 teaspoons of the reserved orange juice or rum. Sift together the flour and a pinch of salt into the mixture, add the raisins and dried bananas, and stir until thoroughly combined.

Put tablespoons of the mixture into mounds on the prepared baking sheets, spaced well apart, then flatten them gently. Bake in the preheated oven for 12–15 minutes, until golden. Let cool on the baking sheets for 5–10 minutes, then, using a metal spatula, carefully transfer to wire racks to cool completely.

Almond Cookies with a Cherry on Top

Makes 25

generous ¾ cup butter,
   cut into cubes, plus extra
   for greasing
½ cup superfine sugar
½ tsp almond extract
2 cups self-rising flour
heaping ¼ cup ground almonds
25 candied cherries (total weight
   about 4½ oz/125 g)

Preheat the oven to 350°F/180°C. Grease several large baking sheets.

Place the butter in a large saucepan and heat gently until melted. Remove from the heat. Add the sugar and almond extract to the pan and stir together. Add the flour and ground almonds and mix to form a smooth dough.

Roll small pieces of the dough between your hands into 25 smooth balls. Place on the prepared baking sheets, spaced well apart, and flatten slightly with your hands, then press a cherry gently into the center of each cookie. Bake in the preheated oven for 10–15 minutes, or until golden brown.

Let cool for 2–3 minutes on the baking sheets, then transfer the cookies to a wire rack to cool completely.

variation
replace the cherries
with dried apricots

Apple Spice Cookies

Makes about 15

1 cup butter, softened

¾ cup superfine sugar

1 egg yolk, lightly beaten

2 tsp apple juice

2 cups all-purpose flour

½ tsp ground cinnamon

½ tsp apple pie spice

pinch of salt

heaping ⅓ cup finely chopped
    plumped dried apple

Filling

1 tbsp superfine sugar

1 tbsp vanilla instant pudding mix

½ cup milk

5 tbsp applesauce

Place the butter and sugar in a large bowl and beat together until light and fluffy, then beat in the egg yolk and apple juice. Sift together the flour, cinnamon, apple pie spice, and a pinch of salt into the mixture. Add the dried apple, and stir until combined. Halve the dough, shape into balls, wrap in plastic wrap, and chill for 30–60 minutes.

Preheat the oven to 375°F/190°C. Line two large baking sheets with parchment paper. Unwrap the dough and roll out between two sheets of parchment paper. Cut out cookies with a 2-inch/5-cm square cutter and place them on the prepared baking sheets, spaced well apart. Bake in the preheated oven for 10–15 minutes, or until light golden brown. Let cool for 5–10 minutes, then transfer to wire racks to cool completely.

To make the apple filling, mix the sugar, pudding mix, and milk together in a saucepan. Bring to a boil, stirring continuously and cook until thickened. Remove the pan from the heat and stir in the applesauce. Cover the surface with plastic wrap and let cool.

Spread the filling over half the cookies and top with the remainder.

Pecan & Maple Cookies

Makes 18

½ cup butter, softened,
    plus extra for greasing

½ cup pecans

2 tbsp maple syrup

scant ½ cup light brown sugar

1 extra large egg yolk,
    lightly beaten

generous ¾ cup self-rising flour

Preheat the oven to 375°F/190°C. Grease two baking sheets. Reserve 18 pecan halves and coarsely chop the rest.

Place the butter, maple syrup, and sugar in a bowl and beat together with a wooden spoon until light and fluffy. Beat in the egg yolk. Sift over the flour and add the chopped pecans. Mix to a stiff dough.

Place 18 golf ball-size spoonfuls of the mixture on the prepared baking sheets, spaced well apart. Top each with a reserved pecan, pressing down gently.

Bake in the preheated oven for 10–12 minutes, until light golden brown. Let the cookies cool on the baking sheets for 10 minutes, then transfer to a wire rack and let cool completely.

variation
replace the maple syrup with honey and the pecans with almonds

Blueberry & Cranberry Cinnamon Cookies

Makes about 30

1 cup butter, softened

scant ¾ cup superfine sugar

1 egg yolk, lightly beaten

2 tsp vanilla extract

2½ cups all-purpose flour

1 tsp ground cinnamon

pinch of salt

½ cup dried blueberries

½ cup dried cranberries

½ cup pine nuts, chopped

Preheat the oven to 375°F/190°C. Line two baking sheets with parchment paper.

Put the butter and sugar into a bowl and mix well with a wooden spoon, then beat in the egg yolk and vanilla extract. Sift together the flour, cinnamon, and a pinch of salt into the mixture, add the blueberries and cranberries, and stir until thoroughly combined.

Spread out the pine nuts in a shallow dish. Scoop up tablespoons of the mixture and roll them into balls. Roll the balls in the pine nuts to coat, then place on the prepared baking sheets, spaced well apart, and flatten slightly.

Bake in the preheated oven for 10–15 minutes. Let cool on the baking sheets for 5–10 minutes, then, using a metal spatula, carefully transfer the cookies to wire racks to cool completely.

Golden Hazelnut Cookies

Makes about 30

1 cup butter, softened

scant ¾ cup superfine sugar

1 egg yolk, lightly beaten

2 cups all-purpose flour

pinch of salt

½ cup ground hazelnuts

To decorate

8 oz/225 g semisweet chocolate,
  broken into pieces

about 30 hazelnuts

Put the butter and sugar into a bowl and mix well with a wooden spoon, then beat in the egg yolk. Sift together the flour and a pinch of salt into the mixture, add the ground hazelnuts, and stir until thoroughly combined. Halve the dough, form into balls, wrap in plastic wrap, and chill in the refrigerator for 30–60 minutes.

Preheat the oven to 375°F/190°C. Line two baking sheets with parchment paper. Unwrap the dough and roll out between two sheets of parchment paper. Stamp out cookies with a 2½-inch/6-cm plain cutter and put them on the prepared baking sheets, spaced well apart.

Bake in the preheated oven for 10–12 minutes, until golden brown. Let cool on the baking sheets for 5–10 minutes, then, using a metal spatula, carefully transfer the cookies to wire racks to cool completely.

When the cookies are cool, place the wire racks over a sheet of parchment paper. Put the chocolate into a heatproof bowl and melt over a saucepan of gently simmering water. Remove the bowl from the heat and let cool, then spoon the chocolate over the cookies. Gently tap the wire racks to level the surface and let set. Add a hazelnut to the center of each cookie.

Lemon & Lime Cookies

Makes about 30

1 cup butter, softened

scant ¾ cup superfine sugar

1 egg yolk, lightly beaten

2 tsp lime juice

2½ cups all-purpose flour

pinch of salt

finely grated rind of 1 lemon

To decorate

5 oz/140 g bittersweet chocolate,
   broken into pieces

30 thinly pared strips
   of lime rind

Icing

1 tbsp lightly beaten egg white

1 tbsp lime juice

1 cup confectioners' sugar

For the decoration, put the chocolate in a heatproof bowl and melt over a saucepan of gently simmering water. Remove from the heat and let cool slightly. Line a baking sheet with parchment paper. Dip the strips of lime rind into the melted chocolate until well coated, then put on the sheet to set.

Put the butter and superfine sugar into a bowl and mix well with a wooden spoon, then beat in the egg yolk and lime juice. Sift together the flour and a pinch of salt into the mixture, add the lemon rind, and stir until thoroughly combined. Halve the dough, shape into balls, wrap in plastic wrap, and chill in the refrigerator for 30–60 minutes.

Preheat the oven to 375°F/190°C. Line two baking sheets with parchment paper. Unwrap the dough and roll out between two sheets of parchment paper to ⅛ inch/3 mm thick. Stamp out rounds with a 2½-inch/ 6-cm plain cutter and put on the baking sheets. Bake in the preheated oven for 10–15 minutes, until golden brown. Let cool for 5–10 minutes, then transfer to wire racks to cool. For the icing, mix together the egg white and lime juice. Gradually beat in the confectioners' sugar until smooth. Spread on the cookies and top with the chocolate-coated lime rind.

Orange & Lemon Cookies

Makes about 30

1 cup butter, softened

scant ¾ cup superfine sugar

1 egg yolk, lightly beaten

2½ cups all-purpose flour

pinch of salt

finely grated rind of 1 orange

finely grated rind of 1 lemon

To decorate

1 tbsp lightly beaten egg white

1 tbsp lemon juice

1 cup confectioners' sugar

few drops yellow food coloring

few drops orange food coloring

about 15 lemon jelly fruit slices

about 15 orange jelly fruit slices

Put the butter and superfine sugar into a bowl and mix well with a wooden spoon, then beat in the egg yolk. Sift together the flour and a pinch of salt into the mixture and stir until thoroughly combined. Halve the dough and gently knead the orange rind into one half and the lemon rind into the other. Shape into balls, wrap in plastic wrap, and chill in the refrigerator for 30–60 minutes.

Preheat the oven to 375°F/190°C. Line two baking sheets with parchment paper. Unwrap the orange-flavored dough and roll out between two sheets of parchment paper. Stamp out cookies with a 2½-inch/ 6-cm cookie cutter and put them on a prepared baking sheet, spaced well apart. Repeat with the lemon-flavored dough but stamp out crescents.

Bake in the preheated oven for 10–15 minutes, until golden brown. Let cool for 5–10 minutes, then transfer to wire racks to cool. To decorate, combine the egg white and lemon juice. Gradually beat in the confectioners' sugar with a wooden spoon until smooth. Spoon half the icing into another bowl. Stir yellow food coloring into one bowl and orange into the other. Spread the icing over the cookies and decorate with the fruit slices. Let set.

Peanut Butter & Jelly Cookies

Makes about 25

1 cup butter, softened

scant ¾ cup superfine sugar

1 egg yolk, lightly beaten

2 tsp vanilla extract

scant ½ cup crunchy
   peanut butter

2½ cups all-purpose flour

pinch of salt

4 tbsp grape jelly

Preheat the oven to 375°F/190°C. Line two baking sheets with parchment paper.

Put the butter and sugar into a bowl and mix well with a wooden spoon, then beat in the egg yolk, vanilla extract, and peanut butter. Sift together the flour and a pinch of salt into the mixture and stir until thoroughly combined.

Scoop out tablespoons of the mixture and shape into balls with your hands, then put them on the prepared baking sheets, spaced well apart. Use the dampened handle of a wooden spoon to make a hollow in the center of each cookie and fill the hollows with grape jelly.

Bake in the preheated oven for 12–15 minutes, until golden brown. Let cool on the baking sheets for 5–10 minutes, then, using a metal spatula, carefully transfer the cookies to wire racks to cool completely.

Iced Cherry Rings

Makes 15–18

½ cup unsalted butter, softened,
    plus extra for greasing

scant ½ cup superfine sugar

1 egg yolk

finely grated rind of ½ lemon

scant 1½ cups all-purpose flour,
    plus extra for dusting

¼ cup candied cherries, finely
    chopped

To decorate

½ cup confectioners' sugar, sifted

1½ tbsp lemon juice

Preheat the oven to 400°F/200°C. Grease two baking sheets.

Cream together the butter and superfine sugar until light and fluffy. Beat in the egg yolk and lemon rind. Sift in the flour, stir, then add the candied cherries, mixing with your hands to a soft dough.

Roll out the dough on a lightly floured surface to about ¼ inch/5 mm thick. Stamp out 3¼-inch/8-cm rounds with a cookie cutter. Stamp out the center of each round with a 1-inch/2.5-cm cutter and place the rings on the prepared baking sheets. Reroll any trimmings and cut more cookies.

Bake in the preheated oven for 12–15 minutes, until firm and golden brown. Let cool on the baking sheets for 2 minutes, then transfer to a wire rack to cool completely.

To decorate, mix the confectioners' sugar to a smooth paste with the lemon juice. Drizzle over the cookies and let set.

Banana & Caramel Cookies

Makes about 30

1 cup butter, softened

scant ¾ cup superfine sugar

1 egg yolk, lightly beaten

2 tbsp finely chopped preserved
   ginger, plus 2 tsp syrup
   from the jar

2½ cups all-purpose flour

pinch of salt

¾ cup finely chopped dried banana

15 chocolate caramel candies

Put the butter and sugar into a bowl and mix well with a wooden spoon, then beat in the egg yolk, ginger, and ginger syrup. Sift together the flour and a pinch of salt into the mixture, add the bananas, and stir until thoroughly combined. Halve the dough, shape into balls, wrap in plastic wrap, and chill in the refrigerator for 30–60 minutes.

Preheat the oven to 375°F/190°C. Line two baking sheets with parchment paper.

Unwrap the dough and roll out between two sheets of parchment paper. Stamp out cookies with a 2½-inch/6-cm fluted round cutter and put half of them on the prepared baking sheets, spaced well apart. Place a chocolate caramel in the center of each cookie, then top with the remaining cookies, and pinch the edges of the cookie sandwiches together.

Bake in the preheated oven for 10–15 minutes, until light golden brown. Let cool on the baking sheets for 5–10 minutes, then, using a metal spatula, carefully transfer to wire racks to cool completely.

Chewy Candied Fruit Cookies

Makes about 30

1 cup butter, softened

scant ¾ cup superfine sugar

1 egg yolk, lightly beaten

2 tsp vanilla extract

2½ cups all-purpose flour

pinch of salt

Candied topping

4 tbsp maple syrup

4 tbsp butter

¼ cup superfine sugar

½ cup chopped plumped dried
  peaches

¼ cup candied cherries, chopped

⅓ cup chopped candied peel

¾ cup chopped macadamia nuts

¼ cup all-purpose flour

Put the butter and sugar into a bowl and mix well with a wooden spoon, then beat in the egg yolk and vanilla extract. Sift together the flour and a pinch of salt into the mixture and stir until thoroughly combined. Halve the dough, shape into balls, wrap in plastic wrap, and chill for 30–60 minutes.

Preheat the oven to 375°F/190°C. Line two baking sheets with parchment paper. Unwrap the dough and roll out between two sheets of parchment paper. Stamp out cookies with a 2½-inch/6-cm plain round cutter and put them on the prepared baking sheets, spaced well apart.

For the topping, put the syrup, butter, and sugar into a saucepan and melt over low heat, stirring occasionally. Meanwhile, put the fruit, candied peel, nuts, and flour into a bowl and mix well. When the syrup mixture is thoroughly combined, stir it into the fruit mixture. Divide the candied topping among the cookies, gently spreading it out to the edges.

Bake in the preheated oven for 10–15 minutes, until firm. Let cool on the baking sheets for 5–10 minutes, then, using a metal spatula, carefully transfer the cookies to wire racks to cool completely.

Walnut & Fig Pinwheels

Makes about 30

1 cup butter, softened

1 cup superfine sugar

1 egg yolk, lightly beaten

2 cups all-purpose flour

pinch of salt

½ cup ground walnuts

1⅔ cups dried figs, finely chopped

5 tbsp freshly brewed mint tea

2 tsp fresh mint, finely chopped

Put the butter and scant ¾ cup of the sugar into a bowl and mix well with a wooden spoon, then beat in the egg yolk. Sift together the flour and a pinch of salt into the mixture, add the ground walnuts, and stir until thoroughly combined. Shape the dough into a ball, wrap in plastic wrap, and chill for 30–60 minutes.

Put the remaining sugar into a saucepan and stir in ½ cup of water, then add the figs, mint tea, and chopped mint. Bring to a boil, stirring continuously, until the sugar has dissolved, then simmer gently for 5 minutes. Remove pan from the heat and let cool.

Unwrap the dough and roll out between two sheets of parchment paper into a 12-inch/30-cm square. Spread the fig filling evenly over the dough, then roll up like a jelly roll. Wrap in plastic wrap and chill for 30 minutes. Preheat the oven to 375°F/190°C. Line two baking sheets with parchment paper. Unwrap the roll and cut into thin slices with a sharp serrated knife. Put the slices on the prepared baking sheets, spaced well apart. Bake in the preheated oven for 10–15 minutes, until golden brown. Let cool on the baking sheets for 5–10 minutes, then transfer to wire racks to cool.

Crunchy Nut & Honey Cookie Sandwiches

Makes about 30

1⅓ cups butter, softened

scant ¾ cup superfine sugar

1 egg yolk, lightly beaten

2 tsp vanilla extract

2½ cups all-purpose flour

pinch of salt

⅓ cup macadamia nuts, cashew nuts, or pine nuts, chopped

¾ cup confectioners' sugar

⅓ cup clover or other honey

Preheat the oven to 375°F/190°C. Line two baking sheets with parchment paper.

Put 1 cup of the butter and the superfine sugar into a bowl and mix well with a wooden spoon, then beat in the egg yolk and vanilla extract. Sift together the flour and a pinch of salt into the mixture and stir until thoroughly combined.

Scoop up tablespoons of the dough and roll into balls. Put half of them on a prepared baking sheet, spaced well apart, and flatten gently. Spread out the nuts in a shallow dish and dip one side of the remaining dough balls into them, then place on the other baking sheet, nut side uppermost, and flatten gently.

Bake in the preheated oven for 10–15 minutes, until light golden brown. Let cool on the baking sheets for 5–10 minutes, then, using a metal spatula, carefully transfer to wire racks to cool completely.

Beat the remaining butter with the confectioners' sugar and honey until creamy and thoroughly mixed. Spread the honey mixture over the plain cookies and top with the nut-coated cookies.

Mango, Coconut & Ginger Cookies

Makes about 30

1 cup butter, softened

¾ cup superfine sugar

1 egg yolk, lightly beaten

3 tbsp preserved ginger, chopped, plus 2 tsp syrup from the jar

2 cups all-purpose flour

pinch of salt

⅓ cup plumped dried mango, chopped

heaping 1 cup dry unsweetened coconut

Place the butter and sugar in a large bowl and beat together until light and fluffy, then beat in the egg yolk and ginger syrup. Sift together the flour and a pinch of salt into the mixture, add the preserved ginger and mango, and stir until combined.

Spread out the coconut in a shallow dish. Shape the dough into a log and roll it in the coconut to coat. Wrap in plastic wrap and chill in the refrigerator for 30–60 minutes.

Preheat the oven to 375°F/190°C. Line two large baking sheets with parchment paper. Unwrap the log, cut it into ¼-inch/5-mm thick slices with a sharp serrated knife, and place them on the prepared baking sheets, spaced well apart.

Bake in the preheated oven for 12–15 minutes, or until light golden brown. Let cool on the baking sheets for 5–10 minutes, then transfer the cookies to wire racks to cool completely.

Crunchy Muesli Cookies

Makes 24

½ cup unsalted butter, softened, plus extra for greasing

½ cup raw brown sugar

1 tbsp honey

heaping ¾ cup self-rising flour

pinch of salt

⅓ cup plumped dried apricots, chopped

heaping ¼ cup dried figs, chopped

1⅓ cups rolled oats

1 tsp milk (optional)

¼ cup golden raisins or cranberries

scant ½ cup walnut halves, chopped

Preheat the oven to 325°F/160°C. Grease two large baking sheets.

Place the butter, sugar, and honey in a saucepan and heat over low heat until melted. Mix to combine. Sift together the flour and a pinch of salt into a large bowl and stir in the apricots, figs, and oats. Pour in the butter and sugar mixture and mix to form a dough. If it is too stiff, add a little milk.

Divide the dough into 24 pieces and roll each piece into a ball. Place 12 balls on each prepared baking sheet, spaced well apart, and press flat to a diameter of 2½ inches/ 6 cm. Mix the golden raisins and walnuts together and press into the cookies.

Bake in the preheated oven for 15 minutes. Let cool on the baking sheets.

variation
top the cookies with
¾ cup mixed nuts before
baking

Peach, Pear & Plum Cookies

Makes about 30

1 cup butter, softened

scant ¾ cup superfine sugar

1 egg yolk, lightly beaten

2 tsp almond extract

2½ cups all-purpose flour

pinch of salt

½ cup finely chopped plumped
dried peach

½ cup finely chopped plumped
dried pear

4 tbsp plum jelly

Preheat the oven to 375°F/190°C. Line two baking sheets with parchment paper.

Put the butter and sugar into a bowl and mix well with a wooden spoon, then beat in the egg yolk and almond extract. Sift together the flour and a pinch of salt into the mixture, add the dried fruit, and stir until thoroughly combined.

Scoop up tablespoons of the mixture, roll them into balls, and put on the prepared baking sheets, spaced well apart. Make a hollow in the center of each with the dampened handle of a wooden spoon. Fill the hollows with plum jelly.

Bake in the preheated oven for 12–15 minutes, until light golden brown. Let cool on the baking sheets for 5–10 minutes, then, using a metal spatula, carefully transfer to wire racks to cool completely.

Peanut Partners

Makes about 30

1 cup butter, softened

scant ¾ cup superfine sugar

1 egg yolk, lightly beaten

2½ cups all-purpose flour

1 tsp ground ginger

pinch of salt

2 tsp finely grated lemon rind

To decorate

3 tbsp creamy peanut butter

3 tbsp confectioners' sugar

whole or chopped roasted
   peanuts

Put the butter and superfine sugar into a bowl and mix well with a wooden spoon, then beat in the egg yolk. Sift together the flour, ginger, and a pinch of salt into the mixture, add the lemon rind, and stir until thoroughly combined. Halve the dough, shape into balls, wrap in plastic wrap, and chill in the refrigerator for 30–60 minutes.

Preheat the oven to 375°F/190°C. Line two baking sheets with parchment paper. Unwrap the dough and roll out between two sheets of parchment paper to about ⅛ inch/3 mm thick. Stamp out cookies with a 2½-inch/6-cm fluted cookie cutter and put them on the prepared baking sheets, spaced well apart.

Bake in the preheated oven for 10–15 minutes, until golden brown. Let cool on the baking sheets for 5–10 minutes, then, using a metal spatula, carefully transfer the cookies to wire racks to cool completely.

Beat together the peanut butter and confectioners' sugar in a bowl, adding a little water if necessary. Spread the cookies with the peanut butter mixture and decorate with whole or chopped peanuts.

Something Special

Chocolate & Ginger Checkerboard Cookies

Makes 30

1 cup butter, softened

scant ¾ cup superfine sugar

1 egg yolk, lightly beaten

2 tsp vanilla extract

2½ cups all-purpose flour

pinch of salt

1 tsp ground ginger

1 tbsp finely grated orange rind

1 tbsp unsweetened cocoa, sifted

1 egg white, lightly beaten

Put the butter and sugar into a bowl and mix well with a wooden spoon, then beat in the egg yolk and vanilla extract. Sift together the flour and a pinch of salt into the mixture and stir until thoroughly combined.

Divide the dough in half. Add the ginger and orange rind to one half and mix well. Shape the dough into a log 6 inches/15 cm long. Flatten the sides and top to square off the log to 2 inches/5 cm high. Wrap in plastic wrap and chill in the refrigerator for 30–60 minutes. Add the cocoa to the other half of the dough and mix well. Shape into a flattened log exactly like the first one, wrap in plastic wrap, and chill for 30–60 minutes.

Unwrap the dough and cut each log lengthwise into three slices. Cut each slice lengthwise into three strips. Brush the strips with egg white and stack them in threes, alternating the flavors, to make the log shapes again. Wrap in plastic wrap and chill for 30–60 minutes. Preheat the oven to 375°F/190°C. Line two baking sheets with parchment paper. Unwrap the logs and cut into slices with a sharp serrated knife. Put the cookies on the baking sheets, spaced well apart. Bake for 12–15 minutes, until firm. Let cool on the baking sheets for 5–10 minutes, then transfer to wire racks to cool.

Neapolitan Cookies

Makes 20

1 cup butter, softened

scant ¾ cup superfine sugar

1 egg yolk, lightly beaten

1 tsp vanilla extract

2½ cups all-purpose flour

salt

1 tbsp unsweetened cocoa

½ tsp almond extract

few drops of green food coloring

1 egg white, lightly beaten

Put the butter and sugar into a bowl and mix well with a wooden spoon, then beat in the egg yolk. Divide the mixture equally among three bowls.

Beat the vanilla extract into the first bowl. Sift together one third of the flour and a pinch of salt into the mixture and stir until combined. Shape into a ball, wrap in plastic wrap, and chill in the refrigerator for 30–60 minutes. Sift together one third of the flour, cocoa, and a pinch of salt into the second bowl and stir. Shape into a ball, wrap in plastic wrap, and chill. Beat the almond extract into the third bowl. Sift together the remaining flour and a pinch of salt and stir. Mix in green food coloring, then form into a ball, wrap in plastic wrap, and chill. Preheat the oven to 375°F/190°C. Line two baking sheets with parchment paper.

Roll out each piece of dough between two sheets of parchment paper to equal-size rectangles. Brush the top of the vanilla dough with egg white and place the chocolate rectangle on top. Brush with beaten egg white and place the almond rectangle on top. Using a sharp knife, cut into ¼-inch/5-mm thick slices, then cut each slice in half. Put on the baking sheets and bake for 10–12 minutes. Let cool for 5–10 minutes, then transfer to wire racks to cool.

Cappuccino Cookies

Makes 30

2 envelopes instant cappuccino

1 tbsp hot water

1 cup butter, softened

scant ¾ cup superfine sugar

1 egg yolk, lightly beaten

2½ cups all-purpose flour

pinch of salt

To decorate

6 oz/175 g white chocolate,
   broken into pieces

unsweetened cocoa, for dusting

Empty the cappuccino sachets into a small bowl and stir in the hot, but not boiling, water to make a paste. Put the butter and sugar into a separate bowl and mix well with a wooden spoon, then beat in the egg yolk and cappuccino paste. Sift together the flour and a pinch of salt into the mixture and stir until thoroughly combined. Halve the dough, shape into balls, wrap in plastic wrap, and chill in the refrigerator for 30–60 minutes.

Preheat the oven to 375°F/190°C. Line two baking sheets with parchment paper. Unwrap the dough and roll out between two sheets of parchment paper. Stamp out cookies with a 2½-inch/6-cm plain cutter and put them on the prepared baking sheets, spaced well apart.

Bake in the preheated oven for 10–12 minutes, until golden brown. Let cool on the baking sheets for 5–10 minutes, then transfer to wire racks to cool. When the cookies are cool, place the wire racks over a sheet of parchment paper. Put the chocolate into a heatproof bowl and melt over a saucepan of simmering water. Remove the bowl from the heat and let cool, then spoon the chocolate over the cookies. Gently tap the wire racks to level the surface and let set. Dust with the unsweetened cocoa.

Spanish Almond Cookies

Makes 15

5½ tbsp unsalted butter, softened, plus extra for greasing

scant ½ cup blanched almonds

scant ½ cup superfine sugar

¼ tsp almond extract

scant ½ cup all-purpose flour

2 extra large egg whites

Preheat the oven to 350°F/180°C. Grease several large baking sheets with butter.

Finely chop the almonds. Place the butter and sugar in a large bowl and beat together until light and fluffy. Add the almond extract, flour, and chopped almonds and stir until thoroughly combined.

Place the egg whites in a large bowl and whisk until soft peaks form and they hold their shape but are not dry. Fold the egg whites into the almond mixture, then place 15 teaspoonfuls of the mixture on the prepared baking sheets, spaced well apart.

Bake in the preheated oven for 15–20 minutes, or until lightly golden brown around the edges. Let cool slightly on the baking sheets for 2–3 minutes, then transfer the cookies to a wire rack to cool completely.

variation
spoon melted chocolate over the cooled cookies and let set

Marshmallow Daisies

Makes 30

1 cup butter, softened

scant ¾ cup superfine sugar

1 egg yolk, lightly beaten

2 tsp vanilla extract

2 cups all-purpose flour

½ cup unsweetened cocoa

pinch of salt

To decorate

about 90 white mini
    marshmallows, halved
    horizontally

4 tbsp peach preserve

4 tbsp yellow sugar sprinkles

Put the butter and sugar into a bowl and mix well with a wooden spoon, then beat in the egg yolk and vanilla extract. Sift together the flour, cocoa, and a pinch of salt into the mixture and stir until thoroughly combined. Halve the dough, roll each piece into a ball, wrap in plastic wrap, and chill in the refrigerator for 30–60 minutes.

Preheat the oven to 375°F/190°C. Line two baking sheets with parchment paper. Unwrap the dough and roll out between two sheets of parchment paper to about ½ inch/1 cm thick and stamp out about 30 cookies with a 2-inch/5-cm flower cutter. Put them on the prepared baking sheets, spaced well apart.

Bake in the preheated oven for 10–12 minutes, until firm. Remove the baking sheets from the oven but do not turn off the heat. Arrange the pieces of marshmallow over the petals of the flowers. Return to the oven for 30–60 seconds, until the marshmallow has softened. Let cool on the baking sheets for 5–10 minutes, then transfer to wire racks to cool. Heat the peach preserve in a small saucepan, strain into a bowl, and let cool. Pipe a small amount of peach preserve in the center of each flower and top with the sugar sprinkles.

Thumbprint Cookies

Makes 36

½ cup unsalted butter, softened

⅔ cup superfine sugar

1 extra large egg, separated

1 tsp vanilla extract

1¼ cups all-purpose flour

pinch of salt

heaping ¼ cup ground almonds

generous ¼ cup seedless
    raspberry jelly

Preheat the oven to 350°F/180°C. Line two large baking sheets with parchment paper. Place the butter and ½ cup of the sugar in a large bowl and beat together until light and fluffy. Add the egg yolk and vanilla extract and beat well to combine. Sift in the flour and a pinch of salt and mix well.

Mix the remaining sugar and the ground almonds together and spread out on a plate. Lightly whisk the egg white in a separate bowl. Roll walnut-size pieces of dough into balls, then dip each ball into the egg white and roll in the almond sugar. Place the balls on the prepared baking sheets, spaced well apart, and make a deep indentation in each cookie.

Bake in the preheated oven for 10 minutes. Remove from the oven, press down again on each indentation, and fill it with jelly. Bake for an additional 10–12 minutes, or until the cookies are golden brown, turning the baking sheets once. Transfer to a wire rack and let cool.

Black & White Cookies

Makes 20

½ cup unsalted butter, softened,
plus extra for greasing

1 tsp vanilla extract

scant 1 cup superfine sugar

2 eggs

2⅔ cups all-purpose flour

½ tsp baking powder

scant 1 cup milk

To decorate

2 cups confectioners' sugar

½ cup heavy cream

⅛ tsp vanilla extract

2¾ oz/75 g semisweet chocolate,
broken into pieces

Preheat the oven to 375°F/190°C. Grease three baking sheets.

Put the butter, vanilla extract, and superfine sugar in a large bowl. Beat the mixture with a whisk until light and fluffy, then beat in the eggs one at a time.

Sift together the flour and baking powder and fold into the beaten mixture, loosening with milk as you work, until both are used up and the mixture drops easily from the spoon.

Drop heaping tablespoonfuls of the mixture on the prepared baking sheets, spaced well apart. Bake in the preheated oven for 15 minutes, until turning golden at the edges and light to the touch. Transfer to wire racks to cool completely.

To decorate, put the confectioners' sugar into a bowl and mix in half of the cream and the vanilla extract until the frosting is thick but can still be spread. Using a metal spatula, spread half of each cookie with white frosting. Melt the chocolate in a heatproof bowl set over a pan of gently simmering water. Remove from the heat and stir in the remaining cream. Spread the dark frosting over the uncoated cookie halves. Let set for 10 minutes before serving.

Fortune Cookies

Makes 12

1–2 tbsp peanut oil, for greasing

2 extra large egg whites

½ tsp vanilla extract

3 tbsp vegetable oil

¾ cup all-purpose flour

1½ tsp cornstarch

pinch of salt

¾ cup superfine sugar

3 tsp water

Write fortune messages on thin strips of paper. Preheat the oven to 350°F/180°C and grease two large baking sheets with a little peanut oil (do not preheat). Place the egg whites, vanilla extract, and vegetable oil in a large bowl, then, using an electric mixer, beat together for 1 minute until frothy but not stiff.

Sift the flour, cornstarch, a pinch of salt, and sugar into a large bowl, stir in the water, and mix. Add the egg white mixture and beat until smooth. Make the cookies in batches of two by spooning 1 scant tablespoon of batter onto each half of the prepared baking sheet and tilting the baking sheet until the batter circles measure 3 inches/8 cm. Bake in the preheated oven for 7–8 minutes, until the edges are beginning to brown.

Work quickly to shape the cookies while still hot. Remove a cookie from the baking sheet with a spatula and fold the cookie in half to form a semicircle. Pinch together at the top and fold the cookie over the rim of a cup. Then insert an index finger into each open end. Bring your thumbs together to press into the middle to form the shape of the fortune cookie. Thread through the strip of paper and place on paper towels to cool. Repeat until all the batter is used.

Traditional Easter Cookies

Makes 30

1 cup butter, softened

¾ cup superfine sugar, plus extra
   for sprinkling

1 egg yolk, lightly beaten

2 cups all-purpose flour

1 tsp apple pie spice

pinch of salt

1 tbsp candied peel

⅓ cup raisins

1 egg white, lightly beaten

Place the butter and sugar in a large bowl and beat together until light and fluffy, then beat in the egg yolk. Sift together the flour, apple pie spice, and a pinch of salt into the mixture, add the candied peel and raisins, and stir until thoroughly combined. Halve the dough, shape into balls, wrap in plastic wrap, and chill in the refrigerator for 30–60 minutes.

Preheat the oven to 375°F/190°C. Line two large baking sheets with parchment paper.

Unwrap the dough and roll out between two sheets of parchment paper. Cut out cookies with a 2½-inch/6-cm fluted round cutter and place them on the prepared baking sheets, spaced well apart.

Bake in the preheated oven for 7 minutes, then brush with the egg white and sprinkle with the sugar. Bake for an additional 5–8 minutes, or until light golden brown. Let cool on the baking sheets for 5–10 minutes, then transfer to wire racks to cool completely.

Turkish Delight Cookies

Makes 30

1 cup butter, softened

scant ¾ cup rose petal-flavored superfine sugar

1 egg yolk, lightly beaten

1 tsp almond extract

2½ cups all-purpose flour

pinch of salt

scant 1 cup chopped pistachios

To decorate

1½ cups pink mini marshmallows, halved horizontally

⅓–⅔ cup dry unsweetened coconut

Put the butter and sugar into a bowl and mix well with a wooden spoon, then beat in the egg yolk and almond extract. Sift together the flour and a pinch of salt into the mixture, add the pistachios, and stir until thoroughly combined. Halve the dough, shape into balls, wrap in plastic wrap, and chill for 30–60 minutes.

Preheat the oven to 375°F/190°C. Line two baking sheets with parchment paper.

Unwrap the dough and roll out between two sheets of parchment paper. Stamp out 2½-inch/6-cm squares and put them on the prepared baking sheets, spaced well apart.

Bake in the preheated oven for 12–15 minutes, until light golden brown, then remove from the oven. Cover the tops of the cookies with halved mini marshmallows. Brush with water and sprinkle with the coconut. Return to the oven for about 30 seconds, until the marshmallows have softened. Let cool on the baking sheets for 5–10 minutes, then, using a metal spatula, transfer the cookies to wire racks to cool completely.

Lavender Cookies

Makes 40

1 cup butter, softened

generous ¾ cup superfine sugar

1 extra large egg, lightly beaten

2¼ cups all-purpose flour

2 tsp baking powder

1 tbsp dried lavender, chopped

Preheat the oven to 375°F/190°C. Line two baking sheets with parchment paper.

Put the butter and sugar into a bowl and mix well with a wooden spoon, then beat in the egg. Sift together the flour and baking powder into the mixture, add the lavender, and stir until thoroughly combined.

Put tablespoons of the mixture on the prepared baking sheets, spaced well apart. Bake in the preheated oven for 15 minutes, until golden brown. Let cool on the baking sheets for 5–10 minutes, then, using a metal spatula, carefully transfer to wire racks to cool completely.

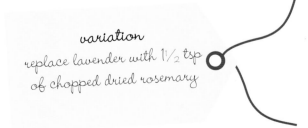

variation
replace lavender with 1½ tsp of chopped dried rosemary

Sugar Cookie Hearts

Makes 30

1 cup butter, softened

scant 1½ cups superfine sugar

1 egg yolk, lightly beaten

2 tsp vanilla extract

2¼ cups all-purpose flour

¼ cup unsweetened cocoa

pinch of salt

To decorate

3–4 food coloring pastes

3½ oz/100 g semisweet
    chocolate, broken into pieces

Put the butter and half the sugar into a bowl and mix well with a wooden spoon, then beat in the egg yolk and vanilla extract. Sift together the flour, cocoa, and a pinch of salt into the mixture and stir until thoroughly combined. Halve the dough, shape into balls, wrap in plastic wrap, and chill in the refrigerator for 30–60 minutes.

Preheat the oven to 375°F/190°C. Line two baking sheets with parchment paper. Unwrap the dough and roll out between two sheets of parchment paper. Stamp out cookies with a heart-shaped cutter and put them on the prepared baking sheets, spaced well apart.

Bake in the preheated oven for 10–15 minutes, until firm. Let cool on the baking sheets for 5–10 minutes, then, using a metal spatula, transfer to wire racks to cool. Divide the remaining sugar among four small plastic bags or bowls. Add a little food coloring paste to each and rub in until well mixed. (Wear a plastic glove to prevent staining.) Put the chocolate in a heatproof bowl and melt over a saucepan of simmering water. Remove from the heat and let cool slightly. Spread the melted chocolate over the cookies and sprinkle with the colored sugar. Let set.

Chocolate Dominoes

Makes 28

1 cup butter, softened

scant ¾ cup superfine sugar

1 egg yolk, lightly beaten

2 tsp vanilla extract

2¼ cups all-purpose flour

¼ cup unsweetened cocoa

pinch of salt

⅓ cup dry unsweetened coconut

scant ⅓ cup white chocolate
   chips

Put the butter and sugar into a bowl and mix well with a wooden spoon, then beat in the egg yolk and vanilla extract. Sift together the flour, cocoa, and a pinch of salt into the mixture, add the coconut, and stir until thoroughly combined. Halve the dough, shape into balls, wrap in plastic wrap, and chill in the refrigerator for 30–60 minutes.

Preheat the oven to 375°F/190°C. Line two baking sheets with parchment paper.

Unwrap the dough and roll out between two sheets of parchment paper. Stamp out cookies with a 3½-inch/9-cm plain square cutter, then cut them in half to make rectangles. Put them on the prepared baking sheets, spaced well apart, and using a knife, make a line across the center of each without cutting through. Arrange the chocolate chips on top of the cookies to look like dominoes, pressing them in gently.

Bake in the preheated oven for 10–15 minutes, until golden brown. Let cool on the baking sheets for 5–10 minutes, then, using a metal spatula, carefully transfer to wire racks to cool completely.

Pear & Pistachio Cookies

Makes 30

1 cup butter, softened

scant ¾ cup superfine sugar

1 egg yolk, lightly beaten

2 tsp vanilla extract

2½ cups all-purpose flour

pinch of salt

½ cup finely chopped plumped
    dried pears

½ cup pistachios, chopped

whole pistachios, to decorate

Preheat the oven to 375°F/190°C. Line two baking sheets with parchment paper.

Put the butter and sugar into a bowl and mix well with a wooden spoon, then beat in the egg yolk and vanilla extract. Sift together the flour and a pinch of salt into the mixture, add the pears and chopped pistachios, and stir until thoroughly combined.

Scoop up tablespoons of the mixture and roll into balls. Put them on the prepared baking sheets, spaced well apart, and flatten slightly. Gently press a whole pistachio into the center of each cookie.

Bake in the preheated oven for 10–15 minutes, until golden brown. Let cool on the baking sheets for 5–10 minutes, then, using a metal spatula, carefully transfer to wire racks to cool completely.

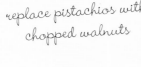

variation
replace pistachios with
chopped walnuts

Carrot Cake Cookies

Makes 30

½ cup butter, softened

scant ½ cup superfine sugar

heaping ⅓ cup light brown sugar

1 extra large egg

½ tsp vanilla extract

heaping 1 cup all-purpose flour

½ tsp baking soda

½ tsp ground cinnamon

¼ cup carrot, finely grated

¼ cup walnut halves, chopped

heaping ¼ cup dry unsweetened
    coconut

Preheat the oven to 375°F/190°C. Line several large baking sheets with parchment paper.

Place the butter and sugars in a large bowl and whisk together until pale and creamy. Whisk the egg and vanilla extract into the mixture until smooth. Sift in the flour, baking soda, and cinnamon, then beat together until well mixed. Add the grated carrot, chopped walnuts, and coconut to the mixture and stir well together.

Drop heaping teaspoonfuls of the mixture on the prepared baking sheets, spaced well apart. Bake in the preheated oven for 8–10 minutes, or until lightly golden brown around the edges.

Let cool on the baking sheets for 2–3 minutes, then transfer to a wire rack to cool completely.

variation
spoon melted chocolate or carob over the baked cookies

Chocolate-Coated Spice Cookies

Makes 60

3 eggs

1 cup superfine sugar

heaping ⅓ cup all-purpose flour

2 tsp unsweetened cocoa

1 tsp ground cinnamon

½ tsp ground cardamom

¼ tsp ground cloves

¼ tsp ground nutmeg

2 cups ground almonds

⅓ cup candied peel,
　　finely chopped

To decorate

4 oz/115 g semisweet chocolate,
　　broken into pieces

4 oz/115 g white chocolate,
　　broken into pieces

sugar crystals

Preheat the oven to 350°F/180°C. Line several large baking sheets with parchment paper. Place the eggs and sugar in a heatproof bowl set over a saucepan of gently simmering water and whisk until thick and foamy. Remove the bowl from the pan and continue to whisk for 2 minutes.

Sift together the flour, cocoa, cinnamon, cardamom, cloves, and nutmeg into the bowl and stir in with the ground almonds and candied peel. Drop heaping teaspoonfuls of the mixture on the prepared baking sheets, spreading them gently into smooth mounds.

Bake in the preheated oven for 15–20 minutes, or until light brown and slightly soft to the touch. Let cool on the baking sheets for 10 minutes, then transfer the cookies to wire racks to cool completely.

Place the semisweet and white chocolates in two separate heatproof bowls, set the bowls over two pans of gently simmering water, and heat until melted. Dip half the cookies in the melted semisweet chocolate and half in the white chocolate. Sprinkle with sugar crystals and let set.

Peach Daiquiri Cookies

Makes 30

1 cup butter, softened

scant ¾ cup superfine sugar

finely grated rind of 1 lime

1 egg yolk, lightly beaten

2 tsp white rum

scant 1 cup chopped plumped
    dried peach

2½ cups all-purpose flour

pinch of salt

To decorate

1¼ cups confectioners' sugar

2 tbsp white rum

Preheat the oven to 375°F/190°C. Line two baking sheets with parchment paper.

Put the butter, superfine sugar, and lime rind into a bowl and mix well with a wooden spoon, then beat in the egg yolk, white rum, and dried peach. Sift together the flour and a pinch of salt into the mixture and stir until thoroughly combined.

Scoop up tablespoons of the dough and put them on the prepared baking sheets, spaced well apart, then flatten gently. Bake in the preheated oven for 10–15 minutes, until light golden brown. Let cool on the baking sheets for 5–10 minutes, then, using a metal spatula, carefully transfer to wire racks to cool completely.

Sift the confectioners' sugar into a bowl and stir in sufficient white rum to give the mixture the consistency of thick cream. With the cookies still on the racks, drizzle the icing over them with a teaspoon. Let set.

Double Heart Cookies

Makes 30

1 envelope instant latte

1½ tsp hot water

1 cup butter, softened

scant ¾ cup superfine sugar

1 egg yolk, lightly beaten

2¼ cups all-purpose flour

salt

1 tsp vanilla extract

3 tbsp unsweetened cocoa

Put the instant latte into a small bowl and stir in the hot water to make a paste. Put the butter and sugar into a bowl and mix well with a wooden spoon, then beat in the egg yolk. Divide the mixture in half. Beat the latte paste into one half. Sift 1¼ cups of the flour with a pinch of salt into the mixture and stir. Shape the dough into a ball, wrap in plastic wrap, and chill in the refrigerator for 30–60 minutes.

Beat the vanilla extract into the other half, then sift together the remaining flour, cocoa, and a pinch of salt into the mixture and stir. Shape the dough into a ball, wrap in plastic wrap, and chill as above.

Preheat the oven to 375°F/190°C. Line two baking sheets with parchment paper. Unwrap both doughs and roll out each between two sheets of parchment paper. Stamp out cookies with a 2¾-inch/7-cm heart-shaped cutter and put them on the prepared baking sheets, spaced well apart. Using a 1½–2-inch/4–5-cm heart-shaped cutter, stamp out the centers of each larger heart and remove. Put a small chocolate-flavored heart in the center of each large coffee-flavored heart and vice versa. Bake for 10–15 minutes. Let cool for 5-10 minutes, then transfer to wire racks to cool.

Chocolate, Date & Pecan Nut Pinwheels

Makes 30

1 cup butter, softened

1 cup superfine sugar

1 egg yolk, lightly beaten

2 cups all-purpose flour

½ cup unsweetened cocoa

pinch of salt

scant 1 cup pecans,
 finely ground

1⅔ cups coarsely chopped
 dried dates

finely grated rind of 1 orange

¾ cup orange flower water

Put the butter and scant ¾ cup of the sugar into a bowl and mix well with a wooden spoon, then beat in the egg yolk. Sift together the flour, cocoa, and a pinch of salt into the mixture, add the pecans, and stir until thoroughly combined. Halve the dough, shape into balls, wrap in plastic wrap, and chill for 30–60 minutes.

Put the dried dates, orange rind, orange flower water, and remaining sugar into a saucepan and cook over low heat, stirring continuously, until the sugar has dissolved. Bring to a boil, then lower the heat and simmer for 5 minutes. Remove the saucepan from the heat, pour the mixture into a bowl, and let cool, then chill in the refrigerator.

Unwrap the dough and roll out between two sheets of parchment paper to rectangles about ¼-inch/5-mm thick. Spread the date filling over the rectangles. Roll up the dough like a jelly roll, wrap in the parchment paper, and chill for 30 minutes more. Preheat the oven to 375°F/190°C. Line two baking sheets with parchment paper. Unwrap the rolls and cut into ½-inch/1-cm slices. Put them on the baking sheets and bake for 15–20 minutes, until golden brown. Let cool on the baking sheets for 5–10 minutes, then transfer the cookies to wire racks to cool.

Margarita Cookies

Makes 30

1 cup butter, softened

scant ¾ cup superfine sugar

finely grated rind of 1 lime

1 egg yolk, lightly beaten

2 tsp orange liqueur or
   1 tsp orange extract

2½ cups all-purpose flour

pinch of salt

To decorate

1¼ cups confectioners' sugar

2 tbsp white tequila

Preheat the oven to 375°F/190°C. Line two baking sheets with parchment paper.

Put the butter, superfine sugar, and lime rind into a bowl and mix well with a wooden spoon, then beat in the egg yolk and orange liqueur or orange extract. Sift together the flour and a pinch of salt into the mixture and stir until thoroughly combined.

Scoop up tablespoons of the dough and put them on the prepared baking sheets, spaced well apart, then flatten gently. Bake in the preheated oven for 10–15 minutes, until light golden brown. Let cool on the baking sheets for 5–10 minutes, then, using a metal spatula, carefully transfer to wire racks to cool completely.

Sift the confectioners' sugar into a bowl and stir in sufficient tequila to produce a mixture the consistency of thick cream. With the cookies still on the racks, drizzle the icing over them with a teaspoon. Let set.

To:
....
....
From:
....
....

Try these tasty:
....
....
Date made:
....
Ingredients:
....
....

Baked for you with love from:

....

Try these tasty:
....
....
Date made:

Ingredients:
....
....

To:
....
....
From:
....
....

Try these tasty:
....
....
Date made:
....
Ingredients:
....
....

Baked for you with love from:

....

Try these tasty:

....

....

Date made:

....

Ingredients:

....

....

To:
....
....
From:
....

Try these tasty:
....
....
Date made:
....
Ingredients:
....
....

Baked for you with love from:

....

Try these tasty:
....
....
Date made:
....
Ingredients:
....
....

To:
....
....
From:
....
....

Try these tasty:
....
....
Date made:
....
Ingredients:
....
....

Baked for you with love from:

....

Try these tasty:

....
....

Date made:

Ingredients:

....
....